DEMCO

THE UKRAINIANS IN AMERICA

The IN AMERICA *Series*

THE UKRAINIANS IN AMERICA

MYRON B. KUROPAS

Published by
Lerner Publications Company
Minneapolis, Minnesota

ACKNOWLEDGMENTS

The illustrations are reproduced through the courtesy of: p. 6, Wasyl Wytwycky; pp. 8 (left and right), 12 (right), 20, 21, 50, 53, 55 (center), 66 (left and right), 68 (top, bottom left and right), Independent Picture Service; p. 9 (bottom), Bill Karpa; pp. 10, 33, Novosti from Sovfoto; p. 11, State Hermitage Museum, Leningrad; pp. 12 (left), 15 (bottom), Culver Pictures, Inc.; p. 13, Slavonic Division, New York Public Library, Astor, Lenox, and Tilden Foundations; pp. 14, 15 (top), Kiev; pp. 17, 23, 25, 30, 36, 40, 59, 63, 72, 73, Ukrainian National Museum, Chicago; pp. 19, 76 (right), 77 (left and right), Cherokee Book Shop; pp. 22, 24, Forum; p. 26, League of Americans of Ukrainian Descent, Chicago, courtesy of Walter Nechay; pp. 27, 31, (left and right), 67, 82 (bottom), The Ukrainian Weekly; pp. 28 (top and bottom), 79 (center), 84, Professor Alexander Granovsky; p. 32, Myron Kuropas; p. 35, United Nations; pp. 38, 43, 47, 51, 54, 69, 71, 74, Dr. Wasyl Halich, author of Ukrainians In The United States; p. 41, Pennsylvania Historical and Museum Commission, Harrisburg, Pennsylvania; pp. 49, 52, The Ukrainian National Association; p. 55 (left), OVID; p. 55 (right), Archbishop Mark J. Hundiak; pp. 60, 61, EKRAN; p. 64, Shevchenko Memorial Committee of America, Inc.; p. 70, The Museum of Modern Art; p. 76, The Museum of Modern Art, Film Department; p. 78, Mary Beck; p. 79 (left), Harvard University, Committee of Ukrainian Studies; p. 79 (right), Georgetown University News Service; p. 80 (left), United States Army; p. 80 (right), Nicholas Minue; p. 82 (top left), New York Rangers; p. 82 (top center), Philadelphia Eagles; p. 82 (top right), Dallas Cowboys; p. 83, Manor Junior College.

LIBRARY OF CONGRESS CATALOGING IN PUBLICATION DATA

Kuropas, Myron B.
    The Ukrainians in America.

    (The In America Series)
    SUMMARY: A history of Ukraine accompanies a discussion of Ukrainians' way of life in and contributions to their new country.

    1. Ukrainians in the United States—Juvenile literature.
    [1. Ukrainians in the United States] I. Title.

E184.U5K8   917.3'06'91791   72-3588
ISBN 0-8225-0221-6

. . . CONTENTS . . .

The Ukrainian Bandurists Chorus of Detroit. Ukrainians have brought their customs and traditions with them to the United States, thereby enriching this nation's cultural heritage.

PART I

Ukraine: Land of the Trident

Ukrainians are one of the few peoples in the world with a national heritage and pride so strong that they have survived centuries of foreign occupation and geographic division but still have preserved a sense of national identity. Beginning in the 13th and 14th centuries, when Ukraine was first conquered by the Poles, Ukrainians have been continually deprived of their national independence by their neighbors.

Ukraine finally achieved independence within recent times, near the end of World War I. In 1918 a Ukrainian National Republic was established, and for a few exciting years the Ukrainian people were free to rule their own land. But in 1921 the Russians regained control of the newly formed state, and once again Ukraine came under foreign rule. However, Ukrainians still have not forgotten their heritage, nor have they given up their desire for independence. Today, as in the past, the Ukrainian people are striving for what they believe are the rights of every nation in the world—self-determination and freedom.

Through the centuries, the symbol of the Ukrainian national heritage has been the trident, a three-pronged spear. Originally used by the rulers of the first Ukrainian state, the trident was adopted as the national seal during the days of the Ukrainian National Republic. Today the trident is used by free Ukrainians everywhere as a reminder to the world that the Ukrainian heritage has not died.

The trident, a three-pronged spear, has been the Ukrainian national emblem since early times. *Left*, a coin dating to the reign of Volodymyr in the 10th century. *Right*, a modern version of the same symbol.

Ukrainians are ethnic descendants of the Slavs, a peaceful agricultural people who for centuries occupied the fertile regions north of the Black Sea, in central Europe. Some time during the first century A.D. the Slavic people, who were divided into many different tribes, began to migrate into other areas of central and eastern Europe. During the centuries that followed, the settlement patterns of these Slavic tribes resulted in the emergence of the Slavic family of nationalities which today includes the Russians, the Ukrainians, the Byelorussians, the Poles, the Slovaks, the Czechs, the Serbians, the Croatians, the Slovenes, and the Bulgarians. Presently, the Russians are the largest Slavic nationality, and the Ukrainians are the second largest.

Situated in the southeastern corner of Europe, the territory in which Ukrainians live is bounded by the Black Sea in the south, the Pripet (Pripyat), Desna, and Seym rivers in the north, the Caucasus Mountains and the Don River in the east, and the southern Dniester River and the Carpathian Mountains in the west. This area includes the regions or provinces known as Great Ukraine, Kuban, Galicia, Volynia, Kholm, and Carpatho-Ukraine. (Carpatho-Ukraine has also been called Carpatho-Russia and Sub-Carpathian Ruthenia.)

The present Ukrainian state, known as the Ukrainian Soviet Socialist Republic (UkSSR), is one of the largest nations of Europe. It covers an area of 232,000 square miles and has a population of 47 million people. The UkSSR is one of the 15 republics of the Union of Soviet Socialist Republics and is bordered by Rumania, Hungary, Czechoslovakia, Poland, Byelorussia, and Russia.

The Ukrainian Soviet
Socialist Republic

Provinces included in the territory inhabited by Ukrainians
(Original map by Bill Karpa)

9

Ukraine is a rich and fertile forest-steppe land which is famous for its agricultural production. Once called the "breadbasket of Europe," Ukraine is one of the world's top producers of rye, wheat, barley, sugar beets, potatoes, corn, and oats. Nature has also endowed the region with an abundance of natural resources, a factor that has in recent years made Ukraine an important industrial arm of the Soviet Union. Coal, oil, salt, manganese ore, and iron ore are some of Ukraine's most valuable assets.

Harvest time on a collective farm in the Ukrainian Soviet Socialist Republic. Ukraine is a fertile farmland once known as the "breadbasket of Europe."

Ukrainians use the Cyrillic alphabet, a Slavic adaptation of the Greek alphabet, in their written language. And, like other Slavic peoples, they have their own language, culture, and history. Ukrainian history is essentially the story of a valiant people, blessed with one of the most productive areas of the world, constantly trying to protect their land from their neighbors.

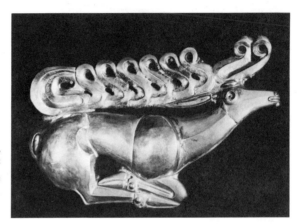

A stag carved in gold by the Scythians, early inhabitants of Ukraine. This carving was done in the seventh or sixth century B.C.

1. *Early History*

Much of what we know about Ukraine's early history we owe to Greek and Roman historians. The ancient Greeks established trading posts along the Black Sea coast as early as the ninth century B.C. Later the Romans used these port cities for their trade. The Greek historian Herodotus gave Ukraine its first historical name. He called it Scythia, after the Scythians, the tribe living in Ukraine at the time the Greeks were trading there.

A variety of European and Asian nomadic peoples occupied the Ukrainian steppes after the Scythians did. The Sarmatians arrived in the third century B.C. and were followed by the Alans in the first century A.D. and the Goths 200 years later. The Goths left out of fear of the Huns, who invaded Ukraine in the fourth century. The Huns remained in southern Ukraine for only a short time and then moved on into Europe. The Slavs arrived during the sixth century, when vast areas of Ukraine were uninhabited.

Volodymyr the Great, who adopted Christianity as the state religion of Kievan Rus in 988

Jaroslav the Wise was known as the "father-in-law of Europe" because his daughters married the kings of Hungary, Norway, and France.

The first recorded Slavic tribe in Ukraine were the Antae. They came as permanent settlers and in time their tribal descendants, each of which came to be known by a different name, had established tribal communities throughout Ukraine. By the ninth century, the most powerful of the Ukrainian-Slavic tribes were the Rus, who settled in the vicinity of the Dnieper River and founded the city of Kiev.

In 879, Kiev was captured by the Varangians (Vikings), and the Rus came under the rule of the Scandinavian royal family of Rurik. Adopting the language, customs, and traditions of the people they conquered, the new Rus rulers began to develop a powerful state. In time the Rus were able to unite all of the Ukrainian-Slavic tribes and to build a vast and powerful empire which came to be known as Kievan Rus.

2. Kievan Rus

Kievan Rus reached the height of its power in the 10th century. Under the wise and popular Volodymyr the Great, the first Ukrainian state was expanded and consolidated. In 988, Volodymyr adopted Christianity as the state religion. He began a massive church and school building program in Kiev, and in time the ancient Ukrainian city became a place of splendor and beauty. In 1017 a visiting German bishop recorded that city possessed over 100 churches and eight trading centers. At the time of Volodymyr's death the empire of Kievan Rus stretched from the Black to the Baltic seas and from the Volga River to the Carpathian Mountains, an area of some 1.2 million square miles.

Another great ruler of Kievan Rus was Jaroslav the Wise, who succeeded Volodymyr. He strengthened Christianity by building churches and monasteries throughout the provinces and by having Kiev recognized as a Metropolitan See (or Archdiocese) by the Eastern Christian Church. Jaroslav also wrote the opening section of the *Ruska Pravda*, the first written code of laws in the Slavic world. Recognized as the ruler of a powerful and cultured state, Jaroslav was able to have his daughters marry the kings of Hungary, Norway, and France.

At this time, the people of Kievan Rus enjoyed an unusual combination of monarchic, aristocratic, and democratic government. Political control of the state was shared by the Prince (the head of the state), the *Druzhina* (a body of royal landowners), and the *Veche* (local councils of representatives elected by free citizens). For the Ukrainian people, this element of democracy is a cherished inheritance from the days of Kievan Rus.

This 14th-century woodcut shows citizens being summoned by a bell to attend the *Veche*, a local council of representatives.

St. Sophia Cathedral in Kiev. This beautiful domed church was built in the 11th century.

After the death of Jaroslav, two events occurred that had an important effect on the course of future Ukrainian history. The first was the division of the Christian church into two separate groups, those who viewed Rome as the major Christian city and those who believed Constantinople to be the Christian capital. As differences between the two groups increased, each side claimed that the other was not truly Christian. In time the eastern church came to be called Orthodox, while the western church was called Catholic. Since the Ukrainian people had received their religious tradition from Constantinople during the reign of Volodymyr, they initially sided with the Orthodox Church.

The other important event occurring after the death of Jaroslav was the gradual decline of Kievan Rus. The decline was largely the result of a series of wars among the royal heirs, who were unable to agree on a common ruler. Eventually the house of Rurik was divided into four separate branches. The first three ruled in Ukraine proper. A fourth branch of the royal family established itself to the northeast, in the vicinity of the Volga River, an area in which the cities of Suzdal, Vladimir, and in time Moscow, were founded.

Detail of St. Sophia Cathedral

In 1169 Andrew Bogolubsky of Vladimir sacked Kiev, and everything of value that could be moved was transported to Vladimir. In 1240 Kiev was sacked again, on this occasion by the heirs of Genghis Khan, the Mongolian warrior chieftain. By this time the Mongols had taken control of the Volga River away from the Suzdalian branch of the old house of Rurik. They ruled Suzdal, Vladimir, and Moscow (which eventually became the state of Muscovy) for almost 250 years.

The Mongol attack on Kiev, 1240

The cultural and linguistic differences which had developed between the ancient Ukrainian tribes and other Slavic tribes, combined with the political division of the house of Rurik, led, in time, to the emergence of three modern nationalities—the Ukrainians, the Byelorussians, and the Russians. Any cultural similarities which existed between the Russian and Ukrainian peoples during the Kievan Rus era came to an end after the fall of Kiev in 1169. The two peoples have progressed along different cultural paths since that time.

3. *Galician-Volynian Rus*

Following the fall of Kiev, the center of Ukrainian national life shifted to the southwest section of the former Kievan Rus state, to the provinces of Galicia and Volynia. By the end of the 12th century, Galicia and Volynia had united to form a separate principality that retained the name Rus. Exposed more and more to the cultural influences of western Europe, this state grew and prospered. Under a series of capable rulers, such as King Daniel (Danylo), who founded the city of Lviv, the political stability of this second Ukrainian state was maintained for over 100 years.

In time, however, Galician-Volynian Rus suffered the same fate as Kievan Rus. Disagreements among royal heirs, combined with the rising power of neighboring states, eventually led to the fall of the second Ukrainian state. In the 14th century, Galicia was conquered by Poland, while Lithuania annexed Volynia and took control of Kiev.

4. *Ukraine in the Polish-Lithuanian Commonwealth*

The Lithuanians were tolerant of the Ukrainians and permitted the development and continued existence of Ukrainian customs and institutions under their rule. Such good fortune was not to last, however. In 1569 Lithuania joined Poland in a commonwealth, and Poland became the dominant power.

The years under Polish rule, both before and after the formation of the commonwealth, were very difficult for Ukrainians. The Polish kings, anxious to unite their empire culturally as well as politically, attempted to eliminate Ukrainian institutions. Things were especially difficult for the Ukrainian Church, then the strongest element of the

King Daniel founded the city of Lviv, naming it after his son Lev. Lviv is also known as I vov (Russian), Lwow (Polish), or Lemberg (Austrian).

Ukrainian national identity. The Polish government levied excessively heavy taxes on Ukrainian churches and when these taxes could not be paid, the churches were closed. With no political state to call their own, and with more and more of their churches being closed, the very existence of the Ukrainian people was now in danger.

Three important developments helped to preserve the Ukrainian heritage during this period. The first was the rise of Orthodox brotherhoods, composed of Ukrainian priests and laymen dedicated to the continued existence of Ukrainian traditions. Mobilizing the Ukrainian people, the brotherhoods raised money, printed books, reopened a number of Ukrainian churches, and organized schools. In these schools, young Ukrainians learned the customs and traditions of their forefathers.

A second important development during this period was the union of the Ukrainian Church with the Catholic Church in 1596. After agreeing that the traditional liturgy and customs of the Ukrainian Orthodox Church, including the right of priests to marry, would remain unchanged, the Pope accepted the Ukrainian Church as part of the Catholic Church. Ukrainians hoped that this would stop the Polish king, who was also Catholic, from interfering with their church. But the king continued to interfere, and some Ukrainian bishops revoked their earlier acceptance of the union, returning to the Orthodox Church. From that day forward, the majority of Ukrainians have belonged to one of two churches—either the Orthodox Church or the Catholic Church.

The third development which helped preserve the Ukrainian heritage during this period was the rise of the Cossack organization, which began soon after the decline of Mongol power in eastern Ukraine. The Mongols gradually retreated from Kiev and its surrounding area as the principality of Muscovy grew in power in the 14th and 15th centuries. This left much of eastern Ukraine uninhabited. A number of adventurous Ukrainians moved into the desolate but richly endowed steppes, first as part-time trappers and hunters and later as permanent settlers. Beginning in the 1500s a number of forts were built along the Dnieper River to protect the settlers from the raids of the Crimean Tartars, descendants of the Mongols living on the Crimean peninsula. Although Poland controlled most of Ukraine politically, it was too weak to protect the Ukrainian settlers, and they were forced to defend themselves. It was in the forts (called *sich* by the Ukrainians) along the Dnieper River that the Cossack way of life was born.

Anyone who accepted the Eastern Orthodox faith was welcome in a sich without question. As each new recruit took his oath of allegiance to the sich, he was given a new name and told to forget his past.

Neither women nor aristocratic titles were permitted in the sich, and the Cossacks recognized no other authority but that of the *hetman* (commander-in-chief) or the *ataman* (commander). Both were elected by the Cossacks in a *rada* (general assembly), and both had to be obeyed without question during military operations. Eventually the Cossacks developed a strong military organization. The emphasis on equality, military discipline, and democratic rule served to make them members of one of the most unusual societies in all of Europe. By the mid-16th century, the Cossacks had formed their own state in southern Ukraine, one that was virtually free from Polish control.

Actor Yul Brynner in a dramatic scene from *Taras Bulba*, a motion picture about the life of the Cossacks

Bohdan Khmelnitsky successfully freed his country from Polish control, but Russia soon took over as ruler of Ukraine.

5. *The Cossack Free State*

The fortunes of the Cossacks between approximately 1550 and 1775 were dependent upon the leadership abilities of individual hetmans and the political situation in Europe. Three hetmans are generally recognized as the most outstanding Cossack leaders. The first of these was Hetman Bohdan Khmelnitsky (or Chmielnicki), whose combined Ukrainian forces defeated the Polish armies in 1648 and established a separate Ukrainian state. In order to have time to build the new nation, Khmelnitsky agreed to a treaty with Muscovy (Russia). The treaty, drawn up in Pereyaslav in 1654, provided for political self-rule in Ukraine. The Russians, however, interpreted the treaty as an invitation to rule and began to station troops in Ukraine soon after the treaty was signed.

Russia's true purpose in Ukraine was recognized by Hetman Ivan Vyhovsky, Khmelnitsky's successor. In 1659, Vyhovsky revoked the Treaty of Pereyaslav and defeated the Russian armies at the Battle of Konotop. He was not able to establish a permanent Ukrainian state, however. The Poles and the Russians, both of whom were opposed to an autonomous Ukraine, decided to come to terms. The Cossacks were too weak to resist both nations and were forced to yield. In 1667,

Poland and Russia partitioned Ukraine along the Dnieper River. Western Ukraine, the "right bank," came under Polish rule, while eastern Ukraine, the "left bank," went to Russia.

A final attempt to unite Ukraine and to establish a permanent Ukrainian state was made by left-bank Hetman Ivan Mazepa 40 years later. Secretly allying himself with Charles XII of Sweden, who was fearful of Russian expansion into Europe, Mazepa planned to rid Ukraine of Russian control. In 1709, however, the combined Swedish and Ukrainian forces were defeated by Czar Peter I at the Battle of Poltava.

Despite the fact that the Cossacks were not successful in their attempts to secure a permanent Ukrainian state, their contribution to the preservation of the Ukrainian national heritage was very important. Fiercely Orthodox, they helped construct churches and supported the work of the Orthodox brotherhoods. The Cossacks also were instrumental in establishing the famous Mohyla Academy in Kiev, which was a leading center of Orthodox scholarship for over 150 years. In terms of the national development of the Ukrainian people,

Ivan Mazepa went to war with Russia in an effort to reestablish a free Ukraine.

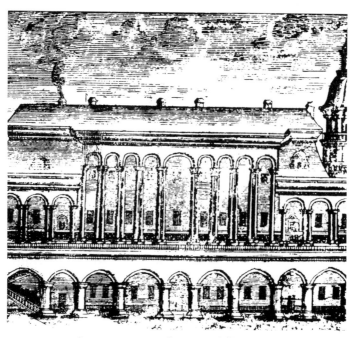

A contemporary drawing of the building which housed the Mohyla Academy

the Cossacks made two important contributions: they revived the democratic tradition of ancient Kiev, and they provided the Ukrainian people with renewed hope for an independent Ukraine.

After the battle of Poltava, Russian military and economic power in central Europe increased rapidly. Poland, weakened from internal strife, fell victim to its powerful neighbors. Three times in the 18th century—in 1772, 1793, and 1796—Poland was partitioned by Prussia, Austria, and Russia. When the third partitioning was completed, Poland ceased to exist. For the next 122 years, Ukraine was ruled by two vast imperial powers, Russia and Austria. Russia controlled eastern Ukraine and part of western Ukraine. Austria controlled three provinces of western Ukraine—Galicia, Bukovina, and Carpatho-Ukraine, all of which had once been part of 11th-century Kievan Rus.

6. *The National Revival*

Life for Ukrainians was as difficult under Russian rule as it had been under Polish rule. The Ukrainian Orthodox Church was officially absorbed by the Russian Orthodox Church in 1686. In 1775 the Zaporozhian Sich, the last remaining Cossack stronghold, was destroyed by the Russian army. In 1781 eastern Ukraine was formally incorporated into the Russian empire, and in 1839 the Ukrainian Catholic Church was also absorbed by the Russian Orthodox Church.

Despite these measures, the Ukrainian national spirit remained alive and, in time, gave birth to a literary and national revival. The literary revival began in 1798, when Ivan Kotlyarevsky (1769-1838) published the *Eneida*, an adaptation of Virgil's *Aeneid* in which the heroes are Ukrainian Cossacks. This book, the first one ever written in the everyday language of the Ukrainian people, made it possible for more Ukrainians to understand the printed word. Kotlyarevsky's initial effort eventually led to a new Ukrainian literary movement.

The height of the Ukrainian literary renaissance was reached in the works of Taras Shevchenko (1814-1861), Ukraine's greatest poet.

Taras Shevchenko and **Ira Aldridge** became friends when Aldridge visited St. Petersburg as part of a Shakespearean troupe.

Born a serf, Shevchenko was a poet of the people, a genius who was able to capture the true sentiment of the Ukrainian nation and to translate it into literary excellence. Severely condemning the Russian czars for their treatment of his people, Shevchenko often thought of the freedom enjoyed by Americans as a result of the War of Independence. Reflecting on the events of 1776, Shevchenko wrote:

> *When will we have a Washington*
> *With a new and a righteous law?*
> *One day we shall have him.*

Several years later, Shevchenko learned about the United States from a first-hand source. One of his close friends was a famous black American, the Shakespearean actor Ira Aldridge. (The two men met when Aldridge was in St. Petersburg as part of a Shakespearean troupe.) Arrested for his views by the czarist police, Shevchenko was forced into military service and sent to a remote camp, where he was forbidden to write. He returned to Ukraine soon after his release from service, but he died a short time later, at the age of 47.

After Shevchenko's works became widely read, the Ukrainian literary revival could not be stopped. The poet's call for freedom was repeated by many other Ukrainian writers, most notably Lesya Ukrainka (1871-1913) of eastern Ukraine and Ivan Franko (1856-1916) of western Ukraine. Fearful lest the Ukrainian people begin to assert their independence in an organized manner, the Russians

Lesya Ukrainka, a Ukrainian writer who took part in the 19th-century national revival

Ivan Franko also contributed to the 19th-century Ukrainian national revival. This painting shows him telling the mountain people of Carpatho-Ukraine about the Ukrainian heritage.

began to take steps to stifle the literary reawakening. In 1863, the Russian Minister of the Interior denied the existence of a separate Ukrainian people, declaring that Ukrainians were really "little Russians" and that their language was actually a Russian dialect. In keeping with this thinking, in 1876 Czar Alexander II issued a proclamation forbidding the publication of all books and materials in the Ukrainian language.

In contrast to eastern Ukraine, where Ukrainians were denied their national identity, Ukrainians living in Austria in the 18th and 19th centuries were permitted some degree of cultural freedom. The Austrians called the Ukrainians living among them "Rusins" (Ruthenians in English) after the ancestral Ukrainian name Rus, and they allowed the Rusins to retain many of their own customs and institutions. The Ukrainian Catholic Church was given special consideration by the Catholic Hapsburgs, the ruling dynasty of Austria. Ukrainian seminaries were established in Vienna, Lviv, and Peremyshl, and Ukrainian parochial schools were created throughout the provinces. Soon there was a group of educated Ukrainians ready to lead their people.

In 1848, Ukrainians in Lviv created the Ruthenian General Council for the purpose of furthering the preservation and development of the Ukrainian national heritage. Later, the council was instrumental

An Easter celebration in 19th-century Bukovina, a province of Ukraine. Religion and religious celebrations have always been a significant part of the Ukrainian national heritage.

in the creation of a number of Ukrainian scientific, cultural, and educational societies. In 1873 the Shevchenko Scientific Society was founded, and in 1882 a Chair of Ukrainian Studies was created at the University of Lviv. Under direction from these two institutions, Ukrainian scholars began to delve into Ukraine's long-buried past and to produce volumes of valuable research material which attested to Ukraine's distinctive cultural and political heritage. Other societies such as *Prosvita* (Enlightenment) and *Sich* worked to improve the life of the Ukrainian peasant through education and cultural activities. Ukrainian reading rooms, libraries, choirs, drama troupes, and social clubs were formed all over Galicia and Bukovina. By 1914 there was hardly a Ukrainian village in either of these two provinces that did not have at least one Ukrainian organization.

The province which benefited the least during this period was Carpatho-Ukraine, an area which had fallen under Hungarian rule during the 11th century. While the peasants had managed to preserve their heritage and language for hundreds of years, the province's intellectual leadership, especially the priests, had become almost totally Hungarian in cultural orientation.

When Hungary came under Austrian rule, the situation improved. A new group of Carpatho-Ukrainian leaders, trained in Ukrainian seminaries in Galicia, began to assert itself. For a time it appeared as if the population of Carpatho-Ukraine would unite with their brothers in Galicia and Bukovina and reestablish their common religious and cultural ties. By 1867, however, Carpatho-Ukraine was once again under Hungarian control. The Ukrainian national revival in Carpatho-Ukraine came to a temporary halt.

7. *The Ukrainian National Republic*

While Ukraine's writers and scholars were laying the cultural foundation for an independent Ukraine, other leaders were preparing the Ukrainian people for liberation. Proposing broad programs of social and national reform, a number of secret Ukrainian political societies came into being in eastern Ukraine between 1846 and 1917.

Michael Hrushevsky was Ukraine's first president.

The Russian Revolution of 1917 overthrew the czar of Russia and gave the Ukrainians an opportunity to establish their independence. After the revolution, a provisional Ukrainian government was quickly organized and an all-Ukrainian Congress was held in Kiev. The Congress, representing all segments of the population of Ukraine, elected a parliament, called the Rada, headed by Professor Michael Hrushevsky (1866-1934).

The front side of a 1917 bill for 100 karbovantsiv, written in the Ukrainian language

The reverse side of the 100-karbovantsiv bill. The language in the upper left-hand corner is Russian; the language in the upper right-hand corner is Polish; and the language at the bottom is Yiddish.

Shortly afterwards the Russian provisional government, ruling in place of the czar, was overthrown by Vladimir Ilytch Lenin, leader of the Russian Communists (Bolsheviks). As new ruler of Russia, Lenin then demanded that the Ukrainian Rada turn over all powers to the Bolsheviks, a minority party in Ukraine. The Rada refused, proclaiming instead the establishment of the Ukrainian National Republic. At the same time, many progressive reforms were introduced. Capital punishment was abolished, all political prisoners were granted their freedom, land was distributed to the peasants, and a new constitution was adopted. Broad provisions guaranteeing the rights of minorities were incorporated into the Ukrainian constitution. In time, three separate cabinet posts were created for each of Ukraine's largest minorities—the Russians, the Poles, and the Jews. Ukrainian paper currency from this period is probably the only money in the world which was printed in four languages—Ukrainian, Polish, Russian, and Yiddish.

The Rada's proclamation was rejected by Lenin, and Russian troops invaded the Ukrainian republic. Realizing that Ukraine's only hope was to pursue an independent international course, the Rada took the final step towards complete freedom from Russia. On January 22, 1918, the Rada declared that from that day forward, the Ukrainian National Republic was "the free sovereign, and independent state of the Ukrainian people." The Ukrainian government then concluded a treaty with Germany and the Central Powers at Brest-Litovsk. Signed in February 1918, the treaty provided that in return for military assistance, Ukraine would supply the Germans with one million tons of foodstuffs. With German and Austrian assistance, the Ukrainian army was able to rid Ukraine of the Bolsheviks. Fighting in Ukraine came to a temporary halt.

The Rada, however, was not able to deliver the promised food supplies to the Central Powers, and it was overthrown by the Germans on April 28. The Ukrainian state was turned over to a group of conservative landowners who established a monarchy headed by Pavlo Skoropadsky (1873-1945). He was proclaimed a hetman, the old title of the Cossack leadership. Despite his lack of popularity among the Ukrainian people, Skoropadsky was an efficient administrator. He built up the Ukrainian treasury, curbed inflation, and supplied the Ukrainian school system with sorely needed funds.

Several months later, in November of 1918, Germany signed the armistice agreement with the Allies, and its troops withdrew from Ukraine. Skoropadsky also left the country. Supporters of the Rada rallied their forces and elected a five-man Directorate, an interim ruling body, headed by Simon Petlura (1879-1926). Petlura reestablished the Ukrainian republic.

Meanwhile, western Ukraine had also moved toward independence. As the war progressed the old Austro-Hungarian empire collapsed. A number of national groups—including the Ukrainians, the Hungarians, the Czechs, and the Poles—began preparing for independence, inspired by President Woodrow Wilson's famous "Fourteen Points," which called for national self-determination. One by one these groups declared their independence.

The city hall in Lviv, where the independence of the Republic of Western Ukraine was proclaimed in 1918

After the German overthrow of the Rada in 1918, **Pavlo Skoropadsky** was proclaimed a monarch by Ukrainian conservatives.

When the Germans were defeated by the Allies, **Simon Petlura** reestablished the Ukrainian republic.

On November 1, 1918, Ukrainians living in the Hapsburg Empire proclaimed the independence of the Republic of Western Ukraine, indicating, at the same time, their desire to unite with Ukrainians in eastern Ukraine. On January 22, 1919, the two Ukrainian republics were formally united. The Ukrainian National Republic now included a geographic area of some 250,000 square miles and a population of over 35 million people.

Despite his best efforts, Simon Petlura could not save the ill-fated Ukrainian National Republic. Three different military forces invaded Ukraine. The Red Russian army, still desiring a Communist regime in Ukraine, reinvaded from the northeast. The czarist (White) Russian army, eager to include Ukraine in a new, non-Communist Russian state, invaded from the southeast. A Polish army, anxious to incorporate the Ukrainian provinces of Galicia and Volynia in the new Polish nation, invaded from the west. Against such overwhelming odds, Ukraine could not survive. The Red Russian army defeated the White Russians and concluded a treaty with Poland, recognizing Poland's claim to Galicia and Volynia. The few remaining companies of the Ukrainian national army were defeated by the Bolsheviks late in 1920, and the Ukrainian National Republic ceased to exist.

A series of treaties concluded by the United States and various European nations in 1919, 1920, 1921, and 1923 partitioned Ukraine further. The province of Bukovina was awarded to Rumania. Carpatho-Ukraine, now called Sub-Carpathian Ruthenia, became a province in Czechoslovakia. Galicia and Volynia remained under Polish jurisdiction. In 1923 eastern Ukraine, now known as the Ukrainian Soviet Socialist Republic, was incorporated into the Union of Soviet Socialist Republics.

The Cathedral of St. George in Lviv. This photograph was taken shortly after World War I.

8. *The Ukrainian Soviet Socialist Republic (UkSSR)*

During the first few years of Communist rule, it appeared as if the UkSSR could maintain some of the cultural and political freedom promised to republics by the Soviet constitution. The Ukrainian Autocephalous (Independent) Orthodox Church and the Ukrainian Academy of Sciences, both founded during the days of the republic, were permitted to continue their work among the Ukrainian people. The Ukrainian school system was strengthened and the Ukrainian language was the only language of instruction. A number of Ukrainian

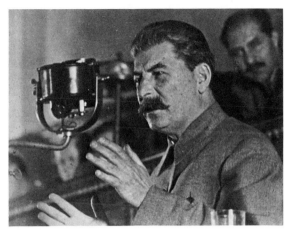

Joseph Stalin in the 1930s. His Russification and collectivization programs caused much hardship among the Ukrainian people.

literary organizations were founded during this period, and Ukrainian books, newspapers, and other periodicals flourished.

But this cultural progress ended soon after Joseph Stalin came to power in the Soviet Union. Between 1929 and 1939, almost 75 percent of the Communist Party leadership in Ukraine was replaced by non-Ukrainians. Ukrainian scientists, scholars, and educators who had attempted to remain independent of Russian control were also replaced. At the same time, the hierarchy of the Ukrainian Autocephalous Orthodox Church was imprisoned and all Ukrainian churches were placed under the jurisdiction of Moscow. Stalin was trying to "Russify" the Ukrainian people.

Hardest hit by the Stalin regime were the Ukrainian peasants. Soon after Stalin took control of the Communist Party leadership, he began a program of industrialization aimed at making the Soviet Union one of the leading industrial powers of the world. To do this, large amounts of money were needed, and Stalin decided to get the money by increasing the Soviet Union's agricultural export market. Individually owned farms were abolished and turned into collective farms. At the same time, the republics in the USSR were assigned agricultural quotas. Every collective in Ukraine and the other republics was required to contribute a certain percentage of its yearly crop to the Soviet government.

By 1932, Ukraine's quota—that is, the percentage of the total harvest that belonged to the state—had been increased to more than

50 percent. When Ukrainians refused to give up so much of their food, the collections were made with the help of the Soviet army. The inevitable result was the worst famine Ukraine had ever experienced. Comparing official Soviet census figures of 1932 with those of 1939, and adding an expected annual population increase of 2.36 percent, indicates that Ukraine had a population loss of 7,465,000 in a seven-year period. About 4,000,000 of this figure was the direct result of the artificially created famine of 1932 and 1933. The remainder of the loss was probably due to deportation of Ukrainians to other parts of the Soviet Union. The deportation program was instituted by Stalin in an attempt to geographically balance the population of the Soviet Union.

World War II temporarily removed Ukraine from Soviet control. Germany invaded Ukraine in 1941. At first, Ukrainians naively believed that Adolf Hitler, ruler of Germany, would help them restore an independent republic. Offering little resistance, many Ukrainians greeted the advancing German army as liberators. Within a few months, however, Hitler's real purpose was revealed; Ukraine was to be a permanent German colony.

The first to feel the brunt of the Nazi occupation were the Jews. No less than 850,000 were killed by the Germans. Of this number, some 50,000 were killed in an infamous ravine called Babi Yar, near Kiev. Nationalist Ukrainian leaders were executed by the thousands, and according to Ukrainian estimates, about 3,000,000 Ukrainians were sent to Germany and Austria to work in factories and forced labor camps.

Resistance against the Nazi occupation by the Ukrainian Partisan Army (UPA) proved to be very costly. UPA attacks on German installations were followed by the execution of hundreds of innocent Ukrainian civilians.

With the help of American military aid, the Soviet army was able to drive the Germans out of Ukraine near the end of the war. By October of 1944 Ukraine was back under Stalin's control. After the war, the regions of Bukovina and Galicia as well as all of Carpatho-Ukraine were incorporated into the Ukrainian Soviet Socialist Republic. Stalin followed the same repressive policies against Ukrainian

The Ukrainian Soviet Socialist Republic delegation at the
United Nations, 1971

nationalist aspirations in the newly acquired Ukrainian provinces as
he had in the older ones.

Despite these measures, however, Stalin insisted that the UkSSR
was an independent state and should be a member of the United
Nations when that body was organized in 1945. In all the years that
Ukraine has been a member of the UN, its representatives have
consistently voted with the Russian delegation.

Conditions in Ukraine improved slightly following the death of
Stalin, especially after Nikita Khrushchev, the new ruler of the Soviet
Union, denounced Stalin's policies. Ukrainian control of the Com-
munist Party of Ukraine increased, and a new generation of young
Ukrainians began to demand a greater voice in the administration of
their republic.

One of the most dramatic developments of the Khrushchev era
was the release, in 1963, of Archbishop-Major Josef Slipyj, from 17
years of forced labor in a Soviet camp in Siberia. Permitted to leave
the Soviet Union, Slipyj was greeted in Rome as a modern-day martyr
for the Christian faith. In 1965, he was elevated to the rank of Cardinal, becoming the fourth Ukrainian to achieve this rank in the
Catholic Church.

Much has changed since 1964, when Khrushchev was succeeded
by Aleksei Kosygin and Leonid Brezhnev. The new Soviet leaders
have muffled dissent and have arrested a number of young Ukrainian
intellectuals who dared to question Moscow's policy in Ukraine. Many

Cardinal Josef Slipyj was released from a Soviet forced labor camp in 1963.

Ukrainians in the free world fear that the present Soviet regime may eventually return to the kind of repression that existed during Stalin's time.

9. *The Future of Ukraine*

Today Ukrainians in the USSR are still seeking greater national freedom within the Soviet Union. And they are still protesting the denial of their human rights. Nor are the Ukrainians alone; other Soviet nationalites and ethnic groups are also dissatisfied.

Ukrainians living in other countries are working to acquaint the world with their country's history. To coordinate their efforts, Ukrainians from 22 countries met in New York City in November of 1967 and created a World Congress of Free Ukrainians. Headed by a General Secretariat, the Congress is expanding its activities to all corners of the world.

Ukrainians in America are also concerned that their fellow Americans know more about Ukraine. An important step in the American effort was reached on July 17, 1959. On that day, Congress passed the so-called Captive Nations Resolution. Recognizing the right of 22 nationalities, including the Ukrainians, to national self-determination, Congress passed a resolution that "the people of the United States share with them their aspirations for the recovery of their freedom and independence." Since that time, the third week of July has been annually designated as Captive Nations Week by Presidents Eisenhower, Kennedy, Johnson, and Nixon.

PART II

Ukrainian Immigration to the United States

1. *Early Pioneers*

Large-scale immigrations of Slavic peoples to America began at a much later date than the immigration of the peoples of western Europe. The Czechs and Poles, the first Slavic groups to make their way to American shores, did not begin their immigration until the first half of the 19th century. And it was not until 1865 that other Slavic groups, among them the Ukrainians, started their move.

However, individual Ukrainians were in America long before the mass immigration. American historical records indicate that people with Ukrainian names were on the North American continent as early as the 17th and 18th centuries. The famous English colonist Captain John Smith, who had been in Ukraine, mentions a man called Lavrenty Bohoon (Bohun) in his memoirs. This same man later accompanied Smith to Jamestown, Virginia.

American Revolutionary War records list a number of Ukrainian names. Little is known of the individuals mentioned, however. The same is true of the early Ukrainian settlers on the west coast. In 1809 Russia established a fortress and colony near San Francisco, California, called Fort Russ (today known as Fort Ross). Among the early settlers of this colony were Ukrainian Cossacks who had been exiled to Siberia and Alaska by the Russian czars.

Historical records also indicate that a number of Ukrainians served in the Union Army during the Civil War. The most famous of these immigrant soldiers was General Basil Turchin, who was a Northern

Ahapius Honcharenko, editor of the *Alaska Herald*

brigade commander in the Battle of Chickamauga. Turchin was born in 1882 in the Don River region of the Russian empire. He graduated from the St. Petersburg Military Academy and rose to the rank of colonel in the Russian Imperial Army. When he emigrated to America, Turchin settled in Illinois. Soon after the start of the Civil War, he accepted a colonel's commission and command of the 19th Illinois Regiment of Infantry Volunteers. Later he was promoted to the rank of brigadier general and became known as the "Terrible Cossack" for his daring military attacks.

Another Ukrainian who contributed to the growth of America was Reverend Ahapius Honcharenko. Born near Kiev in 1832, Honcharenko graduated from the Orthodox Theological Seminary in Kiev. After serving as a priest in that city, he was assigned to the Russian embassy in Athens, Greece, as a resident chaplain. While in Athens, Honcharenko began to speak out against the czar and was arrested by the Russian secret police. Escaping from his captors, he made his way to England, where he continued his verbal and written attacks on the czar.

Honcharenko came to America in 1865 and eventually settled in San Francisco. On March 1, 1868, he began publishing the *Alaska Herald*, a bi-weekly newspaper intended primarily for the Russian and English populations of Alaska and California. With articles in both Russian and English, the *Alaska Herald* helped bridge the cultural gap between the Slavic inhabitants of Alaska and the citizens of the United States. The first issue carried the United States Constitution in Russian. It also had an English translation of the freedom poetry of Taras Shevchenko. A strong supporter of liberty and justice, Honcharenko did not ignore the many injustices which existed in America. In one issue the paper condemned the activities of the infamous Ku Klux Klan, and in another issue it had sharp words for the citizens of San Francisco and their treatment of the Chinese.

While Ahapius Honcharenko played an important role in the history of the 49th state, another Ukrainian, Dr. Nikolai Sudzilovsky (who later changed his surname to Rusel), participated in the political life of the 50th state, Hawaii. Dr. Rusel arrived in San Francisco in the early 1880s and practiced medicine there until 1895, when he moved to Hawaii. In 1896 he helped organize the Hawaiian Medical Society. In 1901 he was elected to the Hawaiian senate, and later he became its presiding officer.

2. Three Periods of Immigration

1870 to 1914

Most Ukrainians who emigrated to America between 1870 and 1914 came from the provinces of Carpatho-Ukraine and Galicia, then under Austro-Hungarian rule. The American Bureau of Immigration called Ukrainians Ruthenians, the name for Ukrainians in Austria,

Many early Ukrainian immigrants came from Carpatho-Ukraine, a beautiful but poverty-stricken region in western Ukraine.

and began to record them as a separate nationality in 1899. According to immigration records, 67,218 Ukrainians came to the United States between 1899 and 1906. Another 187,058 Ukrainians arrived between 1907 and 1914. Taking into account the sizable Ukrainian immigration between 1870 and 1899 (unrecorded) and the fact that after 1899 many immigration officials, unfamiliar with the Ukrainian name, recorded some Ukrainians as Poles, Slovaks, Hungarians, and Russians, these figures are far from accurate. Students of Ukrainian immigration believe that there were at least 500,000 first- and second-generation Ukrainians living in America by 1914.

Most of the Ukrainians who came to America during the first period of immigration were peasant farmers from Austro-Hungary. Despite a certain degree of cultural freedom, life for Ukrainians living under Austro-Hungarian rule was not easy. The average Ukrainian's farm was small, and he could not afford to buy more land. Jobs were not available since there was little industry. Taxes were high and poverty was always near. Under these circumstances, it was difficult to raise the money to travel to America, and at first only a few Ukrainians could afford to make the trip. They raised the necessary amount by selling or renting their land, selling their livestock, and borrowing money from relatives.

Once a few Ukrainians made their way to the United States and wrote to their families and friends about the opportunities in America, the exodus from Austro-Hungary began. Emigration increased so rapidly that at times many villages had more than half of their population preparing to leave for America.

Ukrainian immigrants usually settled where their friends or relatives were already living. Three states—Pennsylvania, New York, and New Jersey—received 85 percent of the Ukrainian immigration during this period. Pennsylvania attracted 113,204 Ukrainian immigrants, which was almost half of those arriving. Other states with sizable Ukrainian populations in 1914 were Ohio, Illinois, Connecticut, Massachusetts, and Michigan.

The majority of the Ukrainians who emigrated to America at this time went to work in the anthracite coal counties of northeastern Pennsylvania. Employed at first as "breaker boys," who separated stones from mined coal, then as miner's helpers, and eventually as full-fledged miners, they labored long and painful hours under often brutal circumstances. Many mining companies seemed more concerned with profit than with the safety of their employees. As a result, mine explosions and cave-ins were hazards that might be encountered at any time. Since there were no unions to bargain over wages and working conditions, the miner was left at the mercy of his employer. It was not uncommon for mining companies to simply lower wages when they wanted to increase their profit margin. Occasionally a

A group of Pennsylvania miners leave their mine in the early morning after having worked underground all night. Pennsylvania coal miners, many of whom were Ukrainians, worked long hours under unhealthy and dangerous conditions.

company would cheat its miners by claiming that they had mined less coal than they actually had. These factors, combined with the high incidence of lung disease among mine workers, made the existence of the Ukrainian miner very difficult. It is not surprising that many a Ukrainian's dream for a better life for himself and his family in America never came true.

Ukrainians who settled in industrial cities also worked long and difficult hours. Their lives, however, were not in such constant danger. These immigrants found employment in the iron and steel industries as well as in glass, rubber, shoe, furniture, automobile, and rail car factories, flour mills, and sugar refining plants. Although wages were generally lower than those offered in the mines, working conditions were better.

One might wonder why Ukrainians, whose European experience was agricultural, did not take up farming in the United States. There were two reasons for this: First, in the last half of the 19th century the United States was experiencing an industrial growth unequaled anywhere in the world. Job opportunities, therefore, were more readily available in industry and in industry-related fields than in agriculture. Second, homestead land, which earlier immigrants had found easy to obtain, was becoming scarce. The Ukrainians who were determined to become farmers in the New World usually went directly to Canada, where a large quantity of land was available, or to the few American states where land was still relatively cheap.

One of the first Ukrainian agricultural communities was founded near Yale, Virginia, in 1892, by a group of Ukrainian Protestants fleeing religious persecution in eastern Ukraine. In 1898 another group of Ukrainian Protestants settled in North Dakota. Other Ukrainians followed, and by 1914 there were more Ukrainian agricultural communities in North Dakota than in any other state. Ukrainians took up farming in several other states, including Georgia, Texas, Illinois, Wisconsin, Michigan, Pennsylvania, New York, and New Jersey.

1920 to 1939

After World War I the United States passed a series of new immigration laws that established quotas for immigrants from southern and

A sod house belonging to a Ukrainian
immigrant in Ukraina, North Dakota

eastern Europe. These laws severely limited Ukrainian immigration to the United States. As a result, no more than 40,000 Ukrainians came to America between the years 1920 and 1939. This period is known as the second immigration. Those who did find their way to the United States usually came from those sections of Ukraine not included in the Ukrainian Soviet Socialist Republic; few Ukrainians were permitted to leave the Soviet Union after 1920.

During this period the center of Ukrainian community life shifted from the anthracite coal regions of Pennsylvania to the large urban areas of the East and Midwest. Six cities—New York, Philadelphia, Pittsburgh, Cleveland, Detroit, and Chicago—emerged as the new centers of Ukrainian-American activity.

After World War II

The post-World War II—or third—Ukrainian immigration was composed largely of individuals who had left Ukraine during the war and who refused to return to the Russian dictatorship ruling their homeland when the war ended. They were permitted to enter the United States under the Displaced Persons Act of 1948. There were approximately 250,000 Ukrainian displaced persons in Europe at the beginning of 1948. With assistance from a number of volunteer agencies, some 85,000 of this number found their way to America. The United Ukrainian American Relief Committee, a charitable organization founded in 1944, had sponsored almost 33,000 Ukrainian immigrants by 1952. Other displaced persons were sponsored by the

National Catholic Welfare Conference as well as by relatives and friends living in the United States. After 1955, another 8,000 Ukrainians, who had originally settled in Poland, Yugoslavia, western Europe, South America, and Australia, emigrated to America.

The third immigration to the United States differed from the earlier immigrations in a number of significant ways. Most pre-World War II Ukrainians, with the exception of the Protestants who were fleeing religious persecution, came to America to escape poverty. But the third immigration came seeking political asylum from Soviet rule. Almost 60 percent of the Ukrainians who came to the United States before 1914 were illiterate, and the Ukrainians who emigrated between the two world wars rarely had had more than five or six years of schooling. On the other hand, most members of the third immigration had at least an eighth-grade education. Many were college graduates and professional people such as doctors, lawyers, engineers, and college professors. A third difference among the three immigrant groups was the fact that a large percentage of the third immigration had been exposed to life in urban areas. As mentioned earlier, most pre-World War II Ukrainian-Americans had emigrated from rural areas. A final difference was the fact that the third immigration to America was greeted by a well-established Ukrainian-American community. The first immigration built the foundation of Ukrainian-American life, the second immigration strengthened it, and the third immigration was able to reap the benefits. Better education, exposure to urban living, and a Ukrainian-American community that was willing to lend moral and financial support—these were all factors which enabled the third immigration to adjust to American life much more quickly than the earlier groups.

Most of the Ukrainians who came to the United States after 1948 settled in the large metropolitan areas of the East and Midwest. The Ukrainian communities of Baltimore, Washington, D.C., and Buffalo, relatively small before the war, grew considerably as a result of the influx. In addition, a number of Ukrainians headed for the South, Southwest, and West, contributing to the growth of Ukrainian communities in Miami, Omaha, Denver, Phoenix, Houston, Los Angeles, and San Francisco.

PART III

The Ukrainian Experience in America

1. *Ukrainians in America Today*

Since census figures do not list Ukraine as a separate land of ethnic origin, it is impossible to determine the exact number of Americans of Ukrainian descent living in the United States today. A fair estimate, however, can be obtained from church affiliation statistics (see tables 1 and 2). On the basis of these figures, it can safely be said that there are at least 500,000 Americans who can trace their ethnic roots to present-day Ukraine. If other groups of Ukrainians are added to this figure—30,000 Ukrainian Protestants, Ukrainians who belong to other churches, and third- and fourth-generation Ukrainians who have completely assimilated into the American mainstream—a final total of between 1,250,000 and 1,500,000 is not inconceivable.

Those Americans who identify themselves as Ukrainian and who are active in the Ukrainian-American community are concentrated in six major metropolitan areas (see table 3). They support 2 daily newspapers (*Svoboda* and *America*), 8 major weekly newspapers, over 50 weekly and monthly periodicals and magazines, 8 national youth organizations, 2 major scholarly societies, 11 professional societies, 3 women's associations, 13 political organizations, and many other local clubs and organizations.

Table 1
Ukrainian Catholic Church Membership

Diocese	Parishes	Clergy	Membership
Philadelphia	99	143	164,000
Stamford	57	103	87,600
Chicago	26	44	30,000

Table 2
Ukrainian Orthodox Church Membership

Church	Parishes	Clergy	Membership
Ukrainian Orthodox Church in the U.S.A.	104	127	87,200
Ukrainian Orthodox Church in America	37	52	40,200

Source: *Ukrainians Abroad* (Toronto: University of Toronto Press, 1971)

Table 3
Estimates of Ukrainian Population in Six Major Metropolitan Areas of the United States, 1970

Area	Estimated Number of Ukrainians
New York	75,000
Chicago	60,000
Philadelphia	50,000
Detroit	45,000
Cleveland	35,000
Pittsburgh	15,000

Based on Ukrainian Fraternal organization membership, church membership, other organizational membership, and Ukrainian press estimates.

2. The Beginning of the Ukrainian-American Community

Organized Ukrainian community life in the United States began in Shenandoah, Pennsylvania, in 1884. In that year America's first Ukrainian Catholic priest, Father Ivan Volansky (1857-1926), emigrated to the United States. A few days after his arrival, Volansky traveled to Philadelphia to present his credentials to the Roman

Catholic Archbishop, Patrick Ryan. But Ryan refused to meet with Volansky and informed him that since Volansky was married it would be best if he returned to Ukraine as soon as possible. Even though the Pope in 1596 had preserved the right of Ukrainian Catholic priests to marry, and even though the Ukrainian Catholic Church was fully recognized by Rome, Archbishop Ryan was not prepared to permit married priests in his diocese. Volansky, reasoning that only his superior in Lviv could end his mission, ignored Archbishop Ryan's suggestion, returned to Shenandoah, and began his work.

The next year the first Ukrainian church in the United States, St. Michael the Archangel, was completed in Shenandoah. In 1886, under Volansky's leadership and inspiration, church building committees were organized in five other Pennsylvania cities (Kingston, Freeland, Olyphant, Shamokin, and Wilkes-Barre) and in Jersey City, New Jersey, and Minneapolis, Minnesota. The following year, after the arrival of Father Lachovych, the second Ukrainian Catholic priest

By 1936, Ukrainians were publishing some 20 newspapers in America.

in America, Volansky left Shenandoah on an extended trip, visiting Ukrainian communities from New York to Minneapolis. Along the way he baptized children, performed marriages, and urged all larger Ukrainian settlements to plan to build a church as the first step in organizing their community.

Volansky's work did not end with church construction. In 1885 he helped organize the Brotherhood of St. Nicholas, the first Ukrainian mutual aid society, or "burial society." The purpose of the society was to provide money for funeral expenses and loans to its members and their families. In 1886, Volansky founded *Amerika*, the first Ukrainian language newspaper in the New World. In 1887, with the help of Volodymyr Simenovych, a young scholar from Lviv, Volansky was able to organize a Ukrainian reading room, instruction classes for illiterates, a choir, and the Cooperative General Store (a self-help enterprise that was owned and managed by Ukrainians). Within two years, this store had branches in five Pennsylvania towns.

Nor did Volansky ignore the everyday problems of the working Ukrainian community. As head of an assembly sponsored by the Knights of Labor, Volansky was regarded as a leading union organizer in Shenandoah during the period that unionism was still in its infancy. In 1888, when a mining strike erupted into violence, it was Volansky, perhaps the only Catholic priest active in the labor movement at this early time, who helped rally the strikers to greater unity in their efforts against unfair labor practices.

3. *Religion*

The Ukrainian Catholic Church

The Ukrainian who emigrated to America in the 19th century brought with him a strong desire to preserve his religious tradition. To him the church represented the fount of his national heritage. For the Ukrainian peasant especially, who was unable to read and was isolated from the Ukrainian national revival for most of the 19th century, there was only one Ukrainian national institution—the church. Ukrainians in America found little religious satisfaction at other Catholic churches—Polish, Slovak, Hungarian—since they were

Father Ivan Volansky, who was the first Ukrainian Catholic priest in the United States, was also the first Catholic priest to be active in the American labor movement.

Latin Rite Catholic. This is not surprising; the Ukrainian Church, although united with Rome, is Byzantine Rite Catholic. In terms of ritual and tradition, little has changed in the Ukrainian Catholic Church since its union with Rome in 1596. Externally, therefore, immigrants found many differences between Latin Rite Catholics and Ukrainian Catholics: Among other things, Ukrainian Catholics had a married clergy, they attended only one kind of service (there were no low and high masses), they bowed rather than genuflected in church, they generally stood during religious services, they made the sign of the cross from right to left, they received Communion under the form of bread and wine (rather than bread alone), they were confirmed immediately after baptism, their liturgical music was more melodic than that in Latin Rite services, and they shunned the use of organs and statues in churches.

In terms of national recognition, Ukrainian immigrants also felt left out. While other nationalities identified themselves by the recognized political existence of their homelands, calling themselves French-Americans, Swedish-Americans, and Irish-Americans, this was not the case with Ukrainians. Ukraine did not exist politically, and few Americans were aware of the Ukrainian heritage. Thus it was natural for the Ukrainian immigrant to believe that the establishment of a Ukrainian Church was the only means of preserving his heritage.

The greatest obstacle to the Ukrainian immigrant's goal was the Latin Rite Catholic Church in the United States. Determined to assimilate all segments of Catholicism in America into one church, the

Interior view of St. Nicholas Ukrainian Catholic Cathedral in Chicago. Unlike Latin Rite Catholic churches, Ukrainian churches usually have paintings rather than statues of holy figures.

Latin Rite hierarchy strongly opposed the formation of separate Catholic parishes on the basis of ethnic origin. This was true of Polish, French, and German parishes as well as Ukrainian ones. Moreover, since all Latin Rite Catholic priests in America were unmarried, American Catholic bishops were strongly against the acceptance of a married clergy in their dioceses. It was against this opposition that the history of the Ukrainian Catholic Church in the United States unfolded.

Father Volansky, "the father of Ukrainian America," was recalled to Lviv in 1889 as a result of pressures on Rome from Latin Rite bishops in America. His work, however, was continued by his successors, some of whom elected to remain celibate in order to avoid friction with American Catholic bishops. More clergy continued to arrive from Ukraine, and the Ukrainian Catholic Church in America began to grow. By 1898, there were 51 functioning churches or chapels.

Conflict between the Ukrainian Catholic clergy and American Catholic bishops continued during this time. In 1889 Father Alexis Toth, a Catholic priest from Carpatho-Ukraine, presented himself to Bishop John Ireland of St. Paul after assuming pastoral duties in Minneapolis. Despite the fact that Toth was a widower and could be considered unmarried, Bishop Ireland refused to accept him into his diocese. In 1891, Toth, still upset over the treatment he had received at the hands of Bishop Ireland, decided to accept the Russian Orthodox faith and the jurisdiction of the Russian Orthodox bishop of San Francisco.

Following his conversion, Toth was given financial assistance from the Russian Orthodox Mission to embark on a campaign to convince other Ukrainians to accept Orthodoxy as the true faith of the Rusin people. "Neither the pope nor the American Catholic Church recognizes our unique status," Toth argued. "If we remain Catholics, we will lose our precious heritage." Since most Ukrainian immigrants were from western Ukraine, they were unfamiliar with the fate of Ukrainian Orthodoxy in eastern Ukraine. There the Ukrainian church had lost its unique status and been absorbed by the Russian Orthodox Church. As a result, Toth's arguments convinced many.

Alarmed by Toth's successes, Ukrainian priests in America as well as the Ukrainian Catholic hierarchy in Europe pleaded with Rome to appoint a Ukrainian bishop in the United States. They saw this as the best way to resolve the conflict with the American Catholic bishops. After a number of unsuccessful attempts to reconcile the differences through other means, the Pope finally agreed and in June of 1907 formally appointed a bishop for American Ukrainians. That same year, Reverend Soter Ortynsky (1866-1916) was elevated to the episcopacy and arrived to take up his duties as the first Ukrainian bishop in the United States.

Soon after his arrival, however, Bishop Ortynsky learned that all of his actions were still subject to the approval of the Latin Rite bishops

An early Ukrainian Catholic church, built in Wilton, North Dakota, in 1907

Bishop Soter Ortynsky, the first Ukrainian Catholic bishop in the United States

in whose dioceses Ukrainian parishes were located. Assisted by the Ukrainian Catholic clergy and by Ukrainian church and lay organizations, Bishop Ortynsky began to ask Rome for greater freedom in his efforts to unify and strengthen the Ukrainian Church in America. In 1913, the Pope responded to the Ukrainian plea by formally establishing a separate exarchate for the Ukrainians. (An exarchate is an administrative church province subject only to the Pope in Rome.) The next year the Pope placed Bishop Ortynsky and his successors on an equal level with American bishops and made all Ukrainian bishops in America subject to no other authority except that of the Holy See. By that time the Ukrainian exarchate included 206 parishes.

Bishop Ortynsky founded an orphanage, organized a new fraternal insurance association, made plans for a Ukrainian seminary, and attempted to unite all elements of the Ukrainian-American Catholic community. Differences existed primarily between the more nationalistic Ukrainian priests from Galicia and the Hungarian-influenced Ruthenian clergy and scholars from Carpatho-Ukraine. Bishop Ortynsky's death in 1916 prevented him from uniting the two groups.

The Ukrainian Catholic Church continued to grow after Bishop Ortynsky's death despite this lack of unity. The Holy See formalized the division in 1924 by nominating two different bishops, one for the Ukrainians from Galicia, and one for the Ruthenians from Carpatho-Ukraine. Bishop Constantine Bohachevsky (1884-1961) succeeded to Bishop Ortynsky's exarchate, while a separate exarchate for Ruthenians was established under Bishop Basil Takach (1879-1948).

Metropolitan Ambrose Senyshyn stands between **Bishop Jaroslav Gabro** and **Bishop Joseph Schmondiuk.** These men head the three dioceses of the Ukrainian Catholic Church in the United States.

Under Bishop Bohachevsky's direction, the Ukrainian Catholic Church in America was placed on a sound financial foundation, new church organizations were established, and the Ukrainian school system was improved. A major concern of the new bishop was the construction of school buildings for full-time elementary day schools for Ukrainian children. The first such school opened in Philadelphia in 1925, and by 1947 there were 18 Ukrainian day schools in addition to the after-school and Saturday schools conducted by most Ukrainian parishes. In the 1930s a number of high schools and junior colleges were also established by the dynamic bishop.

Bishop Bohachevsky's episcopacy, while productive, was not without controversy. In 1929 the Pope gave in to American Catholic pressure and issued a decree that prohibited marriage for all future Ukrainian priests in America. Arguing that a married priesthood was a right guaranteed to the Ukrainian church when it joined the Roman church in 1596, a number of Ukrainian priests urged Bishop Bohachevsky to reject Rome's new directive. And when Bishop Bohachevsky decided to support and enforce the new ruling, some of these priests joined the newly established Ukrainian Orthodox Church.

Most Ukrainian Catholic priests remained loyal to Bishop Bohachevsky, however, and the church was able to survive and flourish. Today, Ukrainian Catholics are divided into three eparchies (dioceses) headed by Metropolitan Ambrose Senyshyn of Philadelphia.

Throughout the years, the Ukrainian Catholic Church in America has been identified as Uniate Catholic, Greek Catholic, Byzantine

Catholic, and even Byzantine-Slavonic Catholic by American Catholics unfamiliar with Ukrainian Catholicism. To avoid such confusion, Ukrainian Catholic bishops from America and Canada met in 1957 and formally adopted Ukrainian Catholic and Ukrainian Rite as the official designations for their church. Today, the Ukrainian Catholic Church enjoys the distinction of being the only wholly national Catholic church in America sanctioned by the Holy See in Rome. What is even more significant, however, is the fact that, with the exception of a married clergy, the basic elements of Ukrainian Catholicism have been preserved.

The Ukrainian Orthodox Church

Ukrainian Orthodoxy in America developed at a much slower pace than Ukrainian Catholicism. This was due to a number of factors. In the first place, an autonomous Ukrainian Orthodox Church in Ukraine was almost nonexistent by the middle of the 19th century; Ukrainian Orthodoxy had been absorbed by Russian Orthodoxy. Secondly, the Ukrainian immigration from eastern Ukraine, where most Ukrainian Orthodox lived, was quite limited prior to 1914. Finally, before 1914 Ukrainians in America who were Orthodox generally were Russian Orthodox; they were former Catholics from western Ukraine who had joined Father Toth's Russian Orthodox parishes in protest over what they believed was Rome's insensitivity to their rights.

An early Ukrainian Orthodox church,
built in Wilton, North Dakota, in 1916

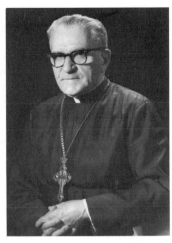

Leaders of the Ukrainian Orthodox Church of America: *Left,* **Metropolitan John Theodoro-vich** (1887-1971); *center,* **Metropolitan Mstyslav Skrypnyk**; *right,* **Archbishop Mark Hundiak**.

Thus it was not until World War I that Ukrainian Orthodoxy began to flourish in the United States. As early as 1915, a group of Ukrainians in Chicago established an independent Ukrainian People's Church. Later, inspired by the establishment of the Ukrainian Autocephalous Orthodox Church in Ukraine in 1920, these pioneers and others with similar religious sentiments began to organize Ukrainian Orthodox parishes.

A Ukrainian Orthodox convention was held in New York City and the independent Ukrainian Orthodox Church of America came into existence. The leaders of the new church proclaimed their unity with the newly formed Autocephalous Orthodox Church in Ukraine. In 1924 the All-Ukrainian Orthodox Council of Ukraine appointed Archbishop John Theodorovich (1887-1971) to be the ecclesiastical administrator of the new religious body in America. Many Ukrainians left the Russian Orthodox Church in the years that followed, and by 1932 Archbishop Theodorovich's diocese included 32 parishes.

Today Archbishop (later Metropolitan) Theodorovich's church, The Ukrainian Orthodox Church of the U.S.A., is the largest Ukrainian Orthodox body in America. Theodorovich passed away in 1971 and was succeeded by Archbishop Mstyslav Skrypnyk.

Ukrainian Protestants

As mentioned earlier, Ukrainian Protestants were in America as early as 1892. Prior to World War II, however, the Ukrainian Protestant movement developed slowly. A Presbyterian parish was established in Newark in 1909. Baptist congregations were established in Scranton in 1904, and in Chicago and Chester, Pennsylvania, in 1915. Between the two world wars, Reverend Basil Kusiw worked on behalf of Ukrainian Protestantism in the United States and Canada, preparing the way for a Ukrainian Protestant revival. After 1950, Baptist congregations were established in Hartford, Cleveland, Philadelphia, Minneapolis, Milwaukee, Pittsburgh, Seattle, and Los Angeles. Today, most Ukrainian Protestants belong to one of two federations — the Ukrainian Evangelical Alliance, headed by Reverend Volodymyr Borowsky, and the Ukrainian Evangelical Baptist Convention, headed by Reverend Olexa Harbuziuk.

4. Education

Another major concern of the Ukrainian immigrants in America has been education. Since most immigrants before 1914 were illiterate, it was necessary to organize adult education classes in which the Ukrainian immigrant could learn to read and write both English and Ukrainian. Most of the classes were conducted in reading rooms or libraries created by individual Ukrainian communities. Reading rooms contained newspapers, books, and pamphlets on topics of general interest. The first reading rooms were organized in the late 1880s, and by 1920 most Ukrainian communities in America maintained at least one such center.

Religious and cultural instruction for Ukrainian youth has also been stressed by Ukrainians in America. The first instruction classes were established in Shamokin, Pennsylvania, in 1893. By 1920, similar classes were in operation in almost every Ukrainian-American locale. Classes were conducted by the priest and the "cantor-teacher." (The cantor in the Ukrainian Catholic Church leads the response to the words of the priest during the services.) In addition to teaching classes in the Ukrainian language, history, geography, culture, and music, the cantor-teacher served as choir director and drama coach. Ukrainian children generally attended these classes between four and six in the evenings five days a week.

With the formation of the Ukrainian Teachers Society in 1913,

Ukrainian youth education in America made several improvements. A coordinated curriculum was devised, a teacher's journal was published, and Ukrainian teaching methods were improved through a series of educational conferences, seminars, and supervisory visits by master teachers. Ukrainian school enrollment rose rapidly between the two world wars.

Today, the Ukrainian school system in America consists of day schools as well as Saturday heritage schools. The Ukrainian Catholic Church operates 33 full-time elementary schools, 5 high schools, and 2 college-level institutions. Most Saturday heritage schools are under the auspices of the Ukrainian Educational Council of the Ukrainian Congress Committee, which is non-denominational and has jurisdiction over 66 such schools. The Ukrainian Orthodox Church operates 36 Ukrainian heritage schools. Children attending heritage schools pursue a 12-year program which includes Ukrainian language, history, geography, literature, and culture. Diplomas, called *matura*, are awarded to all who successfully pass the written and oral examinations given at the completion of the program.

5. *Organizations*

A major concern of the Ukrainian-American community has been to establish strong, self-sustaining organizations which provide a variety of cultural, financial, political, scientific, and recreational programs. These organizations have helped Ukrainians become loyal and patriotic Americans.

Fraternal Insurance Associations

Fraternal insurance associations have two main purposes: They lend financial support to various Ukrainian enterprises in both America and Europe, and they provide death benefits for their members.

The first such association in the United States was Father Volansky's Brotherhood of St. Nicholas. In 1894, following the demise of this association, another insurance society, the Ukrainian National Association, was founded. It is the largest non-sectarian Ukrainian organization in the United States. Today there are three other Ukrainian fraternal associations as well. They include the Ukrainian Workingmen's Association (founded in 1910), the Providence Association of Ukrainian Catholics (founded in 1912), and the Ukrainian National Aid Association (founded in 1915). All are presently enjoying annual increases in membership.

The Ukrainian fraternal insurance associations have served as the financial backbone of the Ukrainian-American community. They also have established reading rooms for illiterates, supported Ukrainian churches and schools, published books, and provided college scholarships. They publish a variety of newspapers and magazines in English and Ukrainian. The fraternal associations have worked to preserve the Ukrainian heritage in America and to lend moral and financial support for Ukrainians in Europe who are striving to establish an independent Ukrainian state.

Financial Institutions

In addition to fraternal insurance associations, Ukrainians have established a number of financial institutions which provide savings facilities, mortgages, loans, and other assistance to Ukrainians and their families.

During the 1920s many Ukrainian communities established savings institutions, several of which have survived until the present. Today there are savings and loan associations in Newark, Philadelphia, Chicago, and Parma (Ohio).

The Self-reliance Association of American Ukrainians was created in 1947. Beginning in 1951, this organization helped establish credit unions in 14 Ukrainian-American communities. Another 8 communities have credit unions with different names.

Political Organizations

Most of the Ukrainian political organizations in the United States have been formed to support the creation of and, after 1920, restoration of an independent Ukrainian state. Prior to World War I, this work was usually initiated by one or all of the Ukrainian fraternal associations then in existence.

Between the two world wars, two organizations, the Hetman Association (*Sich*) and the Organization for the Rebirth of Ukraine

A 1926 photograph of the *Sich* guard in Chicago

(ODWU), were established. Both were national in scope, with branches in most Ukrainian communities, and both held adult education classes, seminars, and national concerts as a part of their activities. Both are still in existence.

A number of Ukrainian political organizations have been established by the third immigration. Among the largest and most active of these are the Organization for the Defense of Four Freedoms in Ukraine (OOCHSU) and DOBRUS (The Democratic Organization of Ukrainians Formerly Persecuted by the Soviet Government).

Youth Organizations

Two youth organizations, *Sokil* and *Sich*, were founded in 1902 as gymnastic societies for young Ukrainian men. The Hetman Association founded a youth affiliate in the 1920s, and a number of new Ukrainian youth organizations were established during the 1930s. The Organization for the Rebirth of Ukraine organized the Young Ukrainian Nationalists (MUN) in 1933. Some 19 MUN branches were in existence by 1939.

Three other youth organizations made their appearance during this time. The largest of these, the Ukrainian Youth League of North America (UYLNA), was founded in 1933. The other two were an Orthodox youth group, now called the Ukrainian Orthodox League

(UOL), and a Catholic youth group, now called the League of Ukrainian Catholics (LUC).

The most active youth organizations in existence today are the Ukrainian Youth Association of America (SUMA), the Ukrainian Scouting Organization, known as *Plast*, and the Organization of Democratic Ukrainian Youth (ODUM), all of which were founded between 1948 and 1950. They offer their members a variety of cultural, social, and athletic activities in Ukrainian communities throughout the United States. And all three own and operate summer camps in New York State and in the Midwest. The main emphasis of these organizations, which now have thousands of members, is on the development of loyal American citizens conscious of their Ukrainian heritage.

Ukrainian students attending American univerisities organized the Federation of Ukrainian Student Organizations of America (SUSTA) in 1953. In 1957, SUSTA initiated a fund for the establishment of a Ukrainian Studies Chair at an American university and, with the help of the Ukrainian-American community, was able to raise over a million dollars for this purpose. On January 22, 1968, exactly 50 years after Ukraine's declaration of independence, Harvard University formally agreed to establish a Center of Ukrainian Studies.

These girls are members of *Plast*, the Ukrainian Scouting Organization in the United States. They are "Yellow Beaks" and have a scouting program similar to that of the Brownies.

A MUN dance group in Chicago

Women's Organizations

The first Ukrainian women's organization, the Sisterhood of St. Olga, was founded in 1897. Many other women's organizations were established in the years that followed. However, most of them are no longer in existence.

The oldest and largest surviving Ukrainian women's organization, the Ukrainian National Women's League of America (UNWLA), was established in 1925. The UNWLA publishes *Our Life*, a monthly journal on topics of interest to Ukrainian women. UNWLA members participate in a variety of community projects, including raising funds for Ukrainian churches and schools, helping needy Ukrainians, and sponsoring cultural concerts and exhibits. An important project has been the preparation of a course of study for preschool Ukrainian children.

Another active Ukrainian women's organization is the Ukrainian Gold Cross, first organized as an affiliate of the Organization for the Rebirth of Ukraine in 1931. The major purpose of this organization is raising funds for needy Ukrainians. Within recent years, however, it has also sponsored cultural activities, children's camps, and preschool centers.

Scientific and Professional Societies

In keeping with the third immigration's interest in scholarship, American branches of the Shevchenko Scientific Society and the

Ukrainian Academy of Sciences were organized after World War II. Both societies are active in research and have published extensively in both the Ukrainian and English languages. A recent accomplishment of the Shevchenko Scientific Society was the compilation of the monumental *Ukraine: A Concise Encyclopedia*, a two-volume work in the English language. It was edited by Dr. Volodymyr Kubijovich and published by the Ukrainian National Association.

In addition to the two scientific societies, there are also professional societies organized by Ukrainian doctors, engineers, teachers, journalists, artists, lawyers, and writers. Of these, the Ukrainian Medical Society, which publishes a medical quarterly, offers scholarships to Ukrainian medical students, and holds annual conventions, is one of the most active.

National Congresses

With so many Ukrainian organizations, it was inevitable that the Ukrainian-American community would begin to coordinate its organizational strength by means of a nationwide federation. There have been three Ukrainian-American federations thus far. The Ukrainian National Council was established in 1915. It was then reorganized into the United Ukrainian Organizations *(Obyednenya)* in the early 1920s. And in 1940 this organization was expanded and renamed the Ukrainian Congress Committee.

Today the Ukrainian Congress Committee, with 61 organizations in its fold, represents 85 percent of the Ukrainians in America. It publishes the *Ukrainian Quarterly* and other special brochures and pamphlets in the English language. Headed by Dr. Lev Dobriansky, a professor at Georgetown University, the Ukrainian Congress Committee has sponsored a number of nationwide projects aimed at informing the world about the Ukrainian freedom crusade.

6. *Milestones in Ukrainian-American History*

In the American experience of every immigrant group, there are certain historic achievements or milestones of which the entire ethnic community can be justly proud. Usually accomplished through great effort and sacrifice by all segments of the community, these milestones

The Ukrainian pavilion at the Chicago World's Fair, 1933

serve as reminders of the achievements that are possible in America when there is unity of effort.

A great moment in Ukrainian-American history was reached by the first immigration. In response to efforts by the Ukrainian National Council, Congress and President Woodrow Wilson proclaimed April 21, 1917, as Ukrainian Day throughout the United States. Thousands of dollars were collected by Ukrainian volunteers standing on hundreds of street corners collecting money for Ukrainian war relief.

Perhaps the greatest single achievement of the Ukrainian-American community between 1920 and 1939 was the Ukrainian pavilion at the World's Fair in Chicago in 1933. Supported by Ukrainian societies and individuals in both Europe and North America, the pavilion was the only fair building in the nationality group not financed by a national government. It included a Ukrainian restaurant, a small stage and open air theater on which Ukrainian dance ensembles and choirs performed, and exhibits featuring Ukrainian folk art, architecture, sculpture, and history. The highlight of the pavilion was a room featuring the works of the world-famous Ukrainian sculptor, Alexander Archipenko.

Another achievement of Ukrainians in America was the erection of the Ukrainian section of the Cultural Gardens in Cleveland, Ohio. The Ukrainian garden, planned and financed under the leadership of Ukrainians in Cleveland, included a statue of Volodymyr the Great and busts of Taras Shevchenko and Ivan Franko, all done by Alexander Archipenko. Dedicated on June 2, 1940, the Ukrainian garden was awarded the first prize among the 15 nationality gardens.

The creation of a Ukrainian Studies Center at Harvard University in 1968 was another milestone in Ukrainian-American history. The center includes professorships in Ukrainian history, literature, and language. In addition to offering doctoral degrees in Ukrainian studies, the center publishes scholarly works, textbooks, and reprints of source materials as part of a continuing publishing program known as the Harvard Series in Ukrainian Studies.

There is one other event within recent times that stands out as a truly significant accomplishment. On June 27, 1965, former President Dwight D. Eisenhower unveiled a statue of Ukraine's beloved poet Taras Shevchenko in Washington, D.C. Speaking to over 100,000 Ukrainians present at the impressive ceremony, Eisenhower said,

> Tyranny and oppression today are not different from tyranny and oppression during the days of Taras Shevchenko. Most of you here today are of Ukrainian descent or origin. All of us, if we go back one generation, or two, or ten, find roots in some other nation, some other country. But today we stand together as Americans, bound by our common devotion to a system of self-government, a system that makes it possible for us to be different and yet united, independent and yet interdependent, diverse and yet inseparable.

The Taras Shevchenko monument in Washington, D.C.

PART IV

Ukrainian Contributions to American Life

All three Ukrainian immigrations have, with the help of the Ukrainian-American community, adapted to the American way of life. Ukrainians have always been loyal and patriotic Americans, sensitive to the needs of their adopted country. This was true even in the days before World War I, when Ukrainians in America were giving major emphasis to the preservation of Ukrainian national traditions. Through its newspaper *Svoboda* (founded in 1893), the Ukrainian National Association urged its members to become American citizens, to participate actively in American civic and political organizations, and to follow the example of great American patriots in their everyday lives. The American Revolution and the rights guaranteed by the Constitution were frequent topics of discussion on the pages of *Svoboda* during that period.

Ukrainians played an important role in the early days of the labor movement in the United States. The example provided by Father Volansky's union activity was followed by several other Ukrainian-American leaders. *Svoboda* was, in many respects, a union newspaper, supporting the efforts of Ukrainian miners to improve their lives. Ukrainian clergymen stood firmly behind the union demands of their parishioners. During an especially long strike in 1900, Father Konstankevych of Shamokin, Pennsylvania, offered to mortgage the Ukrainian church in order to provide funds for striking miners. It was because of the efforts of the Ukrainians and other Slavs that the miners were finally able to organize a strong and effective United Mine Workers union.

1. *Architecture*

The Ukrainian church, traditionally the center of Ukrainian community life, has contributed to the architectural variety and splendor of America. Hundreds of Ukrainian churches can be found throughout the United States, especially in northeastern Pennsylvania and certain sections of North Dakota. Multi-domed and multi-naved in architectural design, most of these churches were built prior to 1920. Early Ukrainian immigrants made every effort to preserve the architectural style of Ukraine in the churches they constructed.

One of the most magnificent Ukrainian churches in America today is St. Nicholas Ukrainian Catholic Cathedral in Chicago. Completed in 1914, St. Nicholas has 13 domes and can seat 1,200 people. There are nine Byzantine-style paintings within the church, many of which are reproductions of mosaic art work found in St. Sophia's Church in Kiev. All of the sketches for the ornamentation of the windows and the altars were planned and drawn by Ukrainian artist and priest Father Hlib Verchovsky. The paintings and most of the decorating

St. Nicholas Ukrainian Catholic
Cathedral in Chicago

St. John the Baptist Ukrainian Catholic
Church in Hunter, New York

were the work of another Ukrainian, Bohdan Katamay, while the entire project was inspired by Father Nicholas Strutynsky, pastor of the church.

The best example of ancient Ukrainian wooden church architecture popular in Carpatho-Ukraine is St. John the Baptist Ukrainian Catholic Church in Hunter, New York. Nestled in the Catskill Mountains, this church was completed in 1962 and is an authentic replica, even to the wooden nails, of similar churches in Ukraine. The architect for this impressive structure was Ivan Zukowsky.

St. Andrew's Ukrainian Orthodox Church-Monument in South Bound Brook, New Jersey. This church, a replica of St. Andrew's in Kiev, is the best example of Ukrainian baroque architecture in the United States.

2. Fine Art

A number of Ukrainian artists have won recognition and acclaim in American and international art circles. Among the best known painters are Edward Kozak, Mykola Butovich, Michael Moroz, and the increasingly popular Lubomyr Hutsaliuk. The work of the talented Oksana Teodorowycz has also received considerable attention. In sculpture, Bodhan Mukhyn, Constantine Milonadis (a master of "kinetic sculpture"), and the versatile Michael Urban are becoming prominent.

Edward Kozak, a Ukrainian artist, came to the United States in 1949.

One of the most popular Ukrainian painters and woodcut artists in America today is Jacques Hnizdovsky. Described by art critics as "a painter of the invisible" and a master of "visual poetry," Hnizdovsky has held exhibitions throughout the world. His works can be found in museums in Philadelphia, Boston, and Cleveland, as well as in the White House and in the private collection of Nelson Rockefeller.

The greatest Ukrainian-American artist was Alexander Archipenko, a sculptor. Born in Kiev in 1887, Archipenko attended the Kiev Art Academy and in 1906, at the age of 19, had his first one-man show.

A woodcut by **Jacques Hnizdovsky**

The Cossack and the Beauty, a painting by **Mykola Butovich**

Alexander Archipenko, world-famous sculptor. His entire career was a search for new ideas, methods, and materials.

Moving to Paris in 1908, he continued his art studies at the École des Beaux Arts. Archipenko's entire artistic career was characterized by a search for new modes of expression. Rejecting the popular Rodin school of sculpture, which portrayed objects realistically, Archipenko first turned to the works of the Cubist painters, especially Pablo Picasso and Georges Braque. In 1913 Archipenko created his famous *Boxers*, recognized today as the first Cubist sculpture and first abstract statue.

Archipenko came to the United States in 1923 and became an American citizen in 1928. In the years that followed, he taught art at the University of Washington, the New Bauhaus School of Industrial Art in Chicago, the University of Kansas City, the University of Oregon, and the University of Delaware. By 1962, he had had 119 one-man exhibitions, and his works could be found in major art museums throughout the world.

Woman Combing Her Hair, a bronze sculpture by Alexander Archipenko in the Museum of Modern Art, New York

Few modern artists have influenced the world of art as much as Archipenko. In addition to pioneering abstract sculpture, he was responsible for a number of other innovations. In 1912 he introduced the concept of sculpto-painting, in which he attached separate parts of a figure onto a plaque in the manner of a relief. Then he painted the entire piece.

Another Archipenko innovation is what has come to be called spatial sculpture. Traditionally, artists believed that sculpture began where the material touched space. Archipenko experimented with the opposite idea by including space within the sculpture. In this new approach the material acts as a frame around the space, giving space an importance of its own.

In the mid-1930s, Archipenko introduced the concept of concave modulation, in which the sculptor makes concave what nature made convex.

Archipenko welcomed the invention of modern materials and readily used them in his art. Working with plexiglass and lucite, Archipenko introduced the idea of light modeling in 1948. His sculpture during this period was a blend of four elements—light, transparency, space, and the concave.

Vasile Avramenko came to the United States in the 1920s and began to teach the historic Ukrainian dances to Ukrainian-Americans. His students have continued to popularize the Ukrainian dance in America.

3. Folk Art

Some of the most important aspects of Ukrainian cultural life in America have been the folk arts, including folk dances and several folk handicrafts.

The man most responsible for popularizing the Ukrainian dance in America was Vasile Avramenko. He came to the United States in the early 1920s and organized over a hundred Ukrainian dance groups. In 1931, some 300 Avramenko-trained Ukrainian dancers appeared at the Metropolitan Opera House in New York. Later, Avramenko dance groups appeared at the Civic Opera House in Chicago and performed for Eleanor Roosevelt on the White House lawn. Today Avramenko's pupils and others are continuing his work throughout the United States.

Ukrainian embroidery is an intricate and beautiful art.

Another folk art which has been preserved in this country is embroidery, a highly developed art form in Ukraine. Used extensively in the Ukrainian church and in Ukrainian dress, the art is practiced by thousands of Ukrainian women in America. One of the acknowledged experts in this field is Oksana Tkachuk of Detroit, an expert in the *nyzynka* stitch, a kind of embroidery popular in Carpatho-Ukraine. Through the years, Mrs. Tkachuk has produced hundreds of embroidered scarves, blouses, doilies, pillow cases, curtains, and drapes.

Easter-egg painting, which dates back to ancient Kievan times, is another popular art practiced by Ukrainian women in America. The Ukrainian Easter egg, or *pysanka*, has become world-famous for its delicate and intricate beauty. While hundreds of Ukrainian women perpetuate this ancient Ukrainian tradition in their home each year, a few have become recognized as masters of the art. Included are Rosalia Rolenka (who began teaching Easter-egg painting in 1915), Eudokia Kushnierchuk, and Wasylyna Kozachok, all of Detroit, and Maria Procai of Minneapolis. A number of American-born Ukrainian women have popularized Ukrainian Easter-egg painting among Americans. The leader in this area is Yaroslava Surmach-Mills.

Wood carving, a highly demanding art form, has also been continued by Ukrainians in the United States. Among the first to introduce this kind of carving to the American public was Severina Parylla, a Ukrainian nun who came to the United States in 1938.

Ukrainian wood carving

4. Music

There is an old saying among Ukrainians, "when two Ukrainians meet, we have the start of another choir." For Ukrainians the song is a second language. The first Ukrainian choir in America was organized in 1887 by Volodymyr Simenovych in Shenandoah, Pennsylvania. From that time on each Ukrainian community has established its own church choir almost as soon as the community was organized. Early choral ensembles sang only during church services, but gradually they expanded their repertoires to include folk songs as well. Eventually a number of choirs began to produce their own musicals.

America came to know Ukrainian music soon after the arrival of the Ukrainian National Chorus, which was formed in the days of the Ukrainian National Republic. Under the direction of Professor Alexander Koshetz, the chorus toured Europe and the United States in 1922 and 1923 and was very well received. So popular did the Koshetz choir become that it was not long before Ukrainian songs were being translated into English. By 1935, Witmark Educational Publications had put out 20 Ukrainian songs. One of these, the beautiful "Carol of the Bells" by Nicholas Leontovych, has since become an American Christmas classic. It was first sung in the United States by the Ukrainian National Chorus.

After the Ukrainian Republic fell and was replaced by Soviet rule, Koshetz and his entire chorus elected to remain in America. Many

73

former chorus members went on to musical fame of their own. Leo Sorochinsky led the Chicago Ukrainian Chorus in two Chicagoland Music Festivals. Competing against top choirs from all over the Midwest, his choir won first place honors in 1930 and 1931. The same chorus won first place again in 1932, this time under the direction of George Benetzky, a former Koshetz chorus member and a tenor with the American Opera Company. The choir took second place in 1933 but managed to recapture first place again in 1934.

Another fine choral group during this period was the Ukrainian Orthodox Church Club of Boston, under the direction of the Reverend Joseph Zelechivsky. Beginning with its participation in Boston's tercentenary celebration, this chorus performed before scores of American audiences as well as on radio in the New England states.

Alexander Koshetz and the Ukrainian National Chorus introduced the "Carol of the Bells" to Americans in the 1920s.

The Ukrainian choral tradition is maintained today by groups organized since the arrival of the third immigration. Among the present day mixed choruses are *Trembita* (Newark), *Kobzar* (Philadelphia), *Dnipro* (Cleveland), *Dumka* (New York City), *Trembita* (Detroit), *Slavuta* (Chicago) and *Surma* (Chicago). One of the most talented of the post-World War II directors was John Zadorozny, who passed away in 1972.

The most outstanding Ukrainian male choir in America today is the Ukrainian Bandurists Chorus of Detroit. Originally organized in Ukraine in 1923, the chorus was reorganized in America in 1949 under the direction of Volodymyr Bozhyk and Hryhory Kytasty. Most of the singers in this unusual musical ensemble accompany themselves on the bandura, the Ukrainian national instrument. Resembling a combination of the lute and the harp, the bandura has 30 to 60 strings and a range of five octaves. Within recent years the Bandurist Chorus has made several tours in the United States, Canada, and Europe.

Another talented bandura chorus is the SUMA Girl Bandurists Ensemble which is under the direction of Peter Potapenko in Detroit. Composed entirely of teen-aged girls, this group has presented more than 100 concerts in the United States and Canada.

A Ukrainian musical milestone came in 1969 when the Ukrainian National Association sponsored an original Ukrainian opera, *Anna Yaroslavna*. The opera is based on the marriage of Anna, daughter of Jaroslav the Wise, to King Henry of France in the 11th century. The music was written by Antin Rudnytsky, and the lyrics by Leonid Poltava.

5. *Entertainment*

Many Ukrainians have achieved recognition in American motion pictures. Anna Sten was the first successful Ukrainian in Hollywood. She appeared in a number of films during the 1930s. John Hodiak was another Hollywood actor of Ukrainian descent. He performed in several amateur Ukrainian theatricals before trying his luck in the professional theater. His first big opportunity came in 1942, when he starred with Tallulah Bankhead in *Lifeboat*. Later he appeared in a variety of movie hits, from the musical *The Harvey Girls* to the war film *A Bell for Adano*. Just before his death in 1955, he appeared on the Broadway stage in *The Caine Mutiny Court Martial*.

Even when he was very young, Nick Adams (born Nicholas Adamchok in Nanticoke, Pennsylvania) wanted to do nothing else except be a Hollywood star. After hitchhiking to Hollywood, he received his first break in the James Dean movie *Rebel Without a Cause*. Later he appeared with Andy Griffith in *No Time for Sergeants*. Just before his death, he starred on his own television series, *The Rebel*.

Measuring six feet six inches tall and weighing 245 pounds, the biggest Ukrainian in Hollywood today is Mike Mazurki. Born in Lviv, Mazurki came to America at the age of six. Invariably cast as a villain or a comic heavy, Mazurki is living proof of the old saying that looks can be deceiving; he is actually a mild-mannered person, a graduate of Manhattan College who speaks four languages and plays the violin. He has appeared in over 125 films, including *Nightmare Alley*, *Donovan's Reef*, *It's a Mad Mad World*, and *Cheyenne Autumn*.

The best known Ukrainian actor today is Jack Palance. Born John Palahniuk in Lattimer Mines, Pennsylvania, Palance has received

Anna Sten

John Hodiak

Mike Mazurki on a movie set
with another actor, Nick Dennis

Jack Palance

wide recognition. His most memorable performances on television were the prize fighter in *Requiem for a Heavyweight* and Mr. Hyde in *Dr. Jekyll and Mr. Hyde*. Among his many film credits are *Shane*, *Barabbas*, *Warriors Five*, *The Big Knife*, and *Che*.

6. Politics

A number of Ukrainian citizens' clubs were created during the early days of the Ukrainian immigration. The purpose of these clubs was to prepare Ukrainian immigrants for citizenship and to teach them the principles of democracy in America.

During the 1890s Ukrainians became active in both major American political parties as Ukrainian affiliates of these parties. Since that time, both the Democrats and the Republicans have had Ukrainian representatives in their nationality divisions (special party divisions for members of ethnic groups).

Although as yet no Ukrainian has served in the United States Congress, Ukrainians have been active in other areas of the government. Ukrainians have been elected to state legislatures in New York, Pennsylvania, Rhode Island, Indiana, and North Dakota. In addition, three Ukrainians have served in federal appointive offices. Joseph

Charyk, president of the Communications Satellite Corporation, was Air Force Under Secretary from 1960 to 1963. Dr. George Kistiakowsky served as a special science advisor to President Eisenhower. Michael Yarymovych was appointed deputy assistant to the Air Force Secretary for Research and Development in 1968.

On the local level, Ukrainians have served as mayors, councilmen, and school board members. One of the best known political figures among Ukrainians is Mary Beck, the first woman ever elected to the Detroit City Council.

Mary Beck

7. Education and Research

Ukrainian contributions to American education and research have been extensive and varied.

Leading the list of prominent Ukrainians in scientific research is Igor Sikorsky, who was born in Kiev. In 1913 Sikorsky built and flew the first successful multi-motored aircraft. After coming to the United States in 1919, he maintained his pioneering interest in aviation and founded the Sikorsky Aviation Corporation. He developed a number of aircraft, including flying boats and the first successful long-range clippers. In fact, trans-oceanic air travel was pioneered by the Sikorsky

Left, **Omeljan Pritsak,** chairman of the Harvard Ukrainian Studies Center. *Center,* **Alexander Granovsky,** professor emeritus at the University of Minnesota, taught entomology for many years. He also has been active in the Ukrainian-American community in Minneapolis-St. Paul. *Right,* **Lev Dobriansky,** president of the Ukrainian Congress Committee, is a professor of economics at Georgetown University.

clippers. In 1939 Sikorsky developed the first successful helicopter in the Western Hemisphere, and in 1941 he established a world's record for sustained helicopter flying. Today Sikorsky is recognized as one of the fathers of the modern helicopter.

Another Ukrainian scientist is Dr. George Kistiakowsky, who was also born in Kiev. Kistiakowsky came to the United States in 1926 and taught chemistry at Harvard University from 1930 to 1960. He is a member of the National Academy of Sciences. As mentioned earlier, in 1960 Kistiakowsky was appointed to serve as President Eisenhower's chief science advisor.

Dr. Stephen Timoshenko's name is well known in the fields of theoretical and applied mechanics, elasticity, and vibration. Born near Kiev in 1878, Timoshenko came to America in 1922. He taught mechanical engineering at the University of Michigan and theoretical and applied mechanics at Stanford University.

Dr. George Vernadsky, professor of history at Yale University, is the most prominent Ukrainian in the social sciences. The son of the first president of the Ukrainian Academy of Sciences in Kiev, Professor Vernadsky came to America in 1927. He has taught at Yale as well as at Stanford, Columbia, and Johns Hopkins universities. His greatest contribution has been in the area of Russian studies. Among his many published works, *Ancient Russia, Kievan Russia, The Mongols and Russia, Bohdan: Hetman of Ukraine,* and his standard one-volume *A History of Russia* are classics.

Dr. Omeljan Pritsak is one of the leading Orientalists in the United States. He is at Harvard University, where he is the chairman of both the Committee on Altaic and Central Asian Studies as well as the Harvard Ukrainian Studies Center.

Many Ukrainian scholars have specialized in Russian and Slavic studies. Of note in this area of research are John Reshetar, author of *The Ukrainian Revolution,* Basil Dmytryshyn, author of *The USSR: A Concise History,* and Yaroslav Bilinsky, author of *The Second Soviet Republic.*

A group of over 100 Ukrainian professors at American universities have formed their own national organization, the Ukrainian-American Association of University Professors. Among other things, the body raises scholarship funds for worthy Ukrainian students.

8. *Military Service*

Ukrainians have served the United States in all of her wars, and many men have been decorated for bravery in action. During World

Left, **Nicholas Minue** was posthumously awarded the Congressional Medal of Honor in 1944. *Right,* **Steve Olek** wears the Ukrainian trident shoulder patch.

War II, Nicholas Minue of Carteret, New Jersey, won the Congressional Medal of Honor for a fearless one-man attack on a German machine gun installation in Tunisia. Completely destroying the German position, Minue continued forward to rout enemy riflemen from dugout positions until he was fatally wounded.

Another outstanding World War II hero was Lieutenant Colonel Theodore Kalakuka, the first Ukrainian graduate of West Point. Assigned to the Philippines, Kalakuka distinguished himself in action by personally saving a wounded soldier during a Japanese air attack, risking his life during another air raid to save valuable medical supplies, and leading an attack on a Japanese landing party after the American company commander was wounded. Captured by the Japanese, Kalakuka died of cerebral malaria in a Japanese prison camp. He was posthumously awarded the Silver Star and two oak leaf clusters.

Following World War II, hundreds of Ukrainian veterans organized Ukrainian VFW and American Legion posts, naming them after Ukrainian-American comrades who had fallen in battle in defense of American freedom. During the Vietnam War, even the Ukrainian trident was brought into combat against America's enemies; at the suggestion of Air Cadet Steve Olek, the 66-C Wing Class at Webb Air Force Base in Texas adopted the trident as their class emblem in 1965. Calling themselves The Flying Cossacks, many members of this class later flew missions in Vietnam wearing the Ukrainian trident shoulder patch.

9. Sports

Ukrainians have excelled in three American sports—hockey, football, and soccer.

In hockey, the famed "Uke" line—Vic Stasiuk, Bronco Horvath, and Johnny Bucyk—made hockey history in the late 1950s. This trio's 1959-60 season was its best, when together these men made an even 200 goals for the Boston Bruins. Bucyk is still a reliable performer for the Bruins and was chosen for the National Hockey League's 1971 All-Star team. Stasiuk is coach of the California Golden Seals. Another outstanding Ukrainian hockey star was Bill Mosienko, who played for

Walter Tkaczuk   **Chuck Bednarik**   **George Andrie**

the Chicago Blackhawks and holds a record for three goals in 21 seconds. Before his death in 1970, Terry Sawchuk was a goaltender for the New York Rangers. He set a record of 103 shut-outs. Dave Balon and Walter Tkaczuk, while playing for the New York Rangers, were part of the National Hockey League's highest scoring line during the 1969-70 season. Eric Nesterenko is a Ukrainian hockey star with the Chicago Blackhawks.

In professional football, the 1930s football hero Bronco Nagurski stands out as one of the greatest fullbacks of all time. Two other well-known Ukrainians in pro ball are Chuck Bednarik, center for the Philadelphia Eagles, and George Andrie, defensive end for the Dallas Cowboys. Bill Malinchak (Detroit), George Tarasovic (Denver), John

Zenon Snylyk, the only player in United States history to have been selected to three U. S. Olympic soccer teams and three World Cup teams

Machuzak (Kansas City), and Don Chuy (Los Angeles) are other Ukrainians who have played professional football. Ukrainians are also found on numerous college football teams every season.

A leading Ukrainian-American soccer star was Zenon Snylyk, who played on the United States Olympic soccer teams in 1956, 1960, and 1964. As a member of the United States World Cup team for a number of years, Snylyk represented his country in 51 matches, an American record. Others who have achieved distinction as members of United States Olympic and World Cup teams are George Kulishenko, Myron Krasij, Jim Stachrowsky, Walter Czyzowych, Walter Schmotolocha,

The Ukrainian Nationals of Philadelphia were United States soccer champions four times in the 1960s.

and Myron Worobec. Two Ukrainian soccer teams have reached the United States national soccer championships: The Ukrainian Nationals of Philadelphia were the champions in 1961, 1962, 1964, and 1966, while the New York Ukrainians captured the U.S. crown in 1965.

In the golf world, Ukrainians are proud of Mike Souchak, a noted golf pro, and Steve Melnyk, the 1969 National Amateur champion. Ukrainians also have a United States senior chess master, Orest Popovych of Brooklyn College of the City University of New York.

Conclusion

If there is a motto that has guided most Ukrainian immigrants and their children it is the one left by Ukraine's poet laureate, Taras Shevchenko, for future Ukrainian generations: "Absorb all cultures but forget not your own." As one of the best organized ethnic groups in America today, Ukrainians have not forgotten their own background after almost 100 years in the United States. Every year on January 22, Ukrainian Independence Day, and on March 14, Shevchenko's birthday, Ukrainians in America renew their resolve to perpetuate their heritage. At the same time, Ukrainians have absorbed all of the beauty and joy of life in a society devoted to freedom and cultural pluralism. Having known tyranny and oppression in their homeland, Ukrainians will never forget the liberty America has given them.

The unique and beautiful Ukrainian Easter egg is one of the many artistic contributions Ukrainians have made to American society. **Maria Procai,** who learned Easter-egg painting from her grandmother in Ukraine, has worked to popularize this art in the United States.

... INDEX ...

ABOUT THE AUTHOR . . .

MYRON B. KUROPAS obtained his B.S. at Loyola University and his M.A. at Roosevelt University in Chicago. Presently he is a Ph.D. candidate at the University of Chicago, where he is writing a dissertation on the Ukrainian immigration.

Mr. Kuropas is employed as the Midwest Regional Director for ACTION, the federal agency which directs the Peace Corps, VISTA, and several other volunteer programs. Formerly he was with the Chicago Public Schools for 15 years, as a teacher, a counselor, and later as a principal. Mr. Kuropas serves on the Board of Directors of the Ukrainian National Association and on the Advisory Committee for the National Project on Ethnic America, an ethnic de-polarization effort of the American Jewish Committee. In addition, he is a member of the President's National Advisory Council on Innovative Education, established to help implement Title III of the Elementary and Secondary Education Act.

A lifelong resident of Chicago, Mr. Kuropas lives in that city with his wife and two sons.

The IN AMERICA *Series*

We specialize in publishing quality books for
young people. For a complete list please write:

LERNER PUBLICATIONS COMPANY
241 First Avenue North, Minneapolis, Minnesota 55401